FUNNY FOOD EXPERIMENTS FOR KIDS

SCIENCE 4TH GRADE

CHILDREN'S SCIENCE EDUCATION BOOKS

Speedy Publishing LLC

40 E. Main St. #1156

Newark, DE 19711

www.speedypublishing.com

Copyright 2017

In this book, we're going to talk about some fun
experiments you can do with food. So, let's get right to it!

There are lots of experiments you can do with simple foods that you can get in the grocery store or may have on hand at home. Make sure that you work with an adult when you perform a science experiment!

EXPERIMENT 1

WHY DO CUT APPLES GET BROWN?

Things you'll need:

You'll need a baking sheet or some wax paper. You'll also need some labeling tape and a pen or marker to use for writing on the tape. You'll need some tongs, a bowl, and a paring knife.

You'll need some foodstuffs too: an apple, a banana, a potato, and an avocado.

Finally, you'll need some different liquids to test: lemon juice, white vinegar, clear soda like Sprite or Seven-Up, olive oil, water, and saltwater.

You may want to take some pictures with your camera or cell phone to substantiate your claims!

What to do:

Step 1: Using the tape, create a different label for each
of the liquids you'll use for the experiment.

Step 2: Put the labels down on the wax paper or the baking sheet. This is the surface you'll use to study the samples you complete during the experiment.

Step 3: Have an adult help you cut each fruit or veggie into slices about 1 centimeter in thickness. For each one, you'll need at least 7 slices, one for each liquid you're testing plus one that will act as a control piece.

Step 4: Put out one slice of each type of food under the "Control" label.

Step 5: Put enough liquid in the bowl so that you can submerge each sample completely under the liquid.

Step 6: Dip each piece of fruit or vegetable into the liquid by using the tongs. Be sure the whole slice gets dipped! When you pull it out, make sure the extra liquid drips off. Then, you can place it next to the label for the liquid you used.

Step 7: Once you've finished testing those four pieces of the apple, banana, potato, and avocado, rinse out the bowl and tongs and then try the second liquid.

Step 8: When you are finished you should have 4 x 6 or 24 different slices. Four slices of different fruits and veggies for each of the 6 liquids you're trying. You'll also have the four control pieces too.

Step 9: Record what you observe and make a note of what time it is. You can use your camera to take pictures of how brown the food gets over time.

You've probably noticed before that when you've taken a bite out of an apple, it begins to turn brown on the inside quite quickly. An enzyme reacts with the air's oxygen and the cofactor inside the "meat" of the fruit. A cofactor of iron or sometimes copper causes the reaction. The fruit begins the process of oxidation, which means the electrons in its atoms are grabbed up by the molecules in the air. This makes the food turn a brownish color. In other words, you can think of it like a form of rust that's edible.

To prevent this from happening, you can cook the fruit, cover it so that air doesn't get to its surface, or make its surface more acidic by dipping it in different acidic liquids, such as lemon juice. These acidic liquids prevent the slices from browning because they have a reaction with the oxygen in the air. After a time, the liquid will finish the process of reacting or it will dry or wash off. Then the sample will get brown. Which liquid was the best at preventing the browning? If you got the answer "lemon juice," you're correct! The control fruit is important so you can see what happens when you don't use any liquid at all.

EXPERIMENT 2

PINEAPPLE AND GELATIN, FRIENDS OR FOES?

Things you'll need:

You're going to need a fresh pineapple and two bowls. You'll also need a cup for measuring, a kettle, a spoon, two quarters, and two packages of gelatin powder. You'll also need some water.

What to do:

Step 1: Get an adult to help you heat some hot water on the stove in a kettle. Use the directions on the gelatin packages to mix the gelatin with hot water.

Step 2: Put an equal amount of the mixed gelatin into two small bowls.

Step 3: Put about ten tiny chunks of the pineapple into bowl #1. Don't put anything else in bowl #2.

Step 4: Place both of the bowls on a shelf in your
refrigerator.

Step 5: Do you think that the pineapple chunks will affect the gelatin or not? Form your hypothesis.

Step 6: Wait for 3 or 4 hours. Then take both bowls of gelatin and place a quarter on top of the surface of the gelatin in each one. Shake the bowls a little from side to side. What happens with bowl #1? What about bowl #2?

The science behind it:

The gelatin that has the pineapple in it doesn't get solid.
The control gelatin, which didn't have any pineapple,
got solid and isn't watery.

Pineapples are really amazing plants. They don't grow on trees. Instead, they grow on a plant that is close to the ground and have very spiky leaves. Pineapples have a type of enzyme that's known as bromelain. This enzyme digests proteins so it's sometimes used as a meat tenderizer! In fact, some people find it irritating to their lips and tongue because it tenderizes them! It's not dangerous if you're eating it, once it gets into your stomach it isn't a problem.

Gelatin is made from the protein of animals, especially collagen. When you mix water and gelatin together long protein molecules form, which you can't see but are part of its structure. Water gets trapped in these chains of molecules and it turns the liquid into squishy gelatin. When the pineapple enzyme mixes with it, it starts to eat the protein so it prevents the gelatin from getting solid. Don't eat this experiment when you're finished because you placed the quarters in them to test them. You can have some fresh pineapple for a snack instead!

EXPERIMENT 3

Things you'll need:

You'll need five rock-hard avocadoes. You'll also need a banana and an apple. You'll need three small brown paper bags and access to a shelf in a refrigerator. A camera or smart-phone so you can take snapshots of your avocadoes is a help for keeping a record of how they looked before the experiment starts.

Step 1: Take pictures of each of your avocadoes.

Step 2: Place avocado #1 on your kitchen counter.

Step 3: Place avocado #2 on a refrigerator shelf.

Step 5: Place avocado #4 inside a bag along with an apple.

Step 7: Don't forget to keep a record of the day you started your experiment.

Step 8: Check your avocadoes after day 1, day 3, day 5, day 7, day 10, and day 14 and record your results in a chart.

Time	Fridge	Kitchen Counter	Plain Bag	Bag with Apple	Bag with Banana
Day 1 Results:					
Day 3 Results:					
Day 5 Results:					
Day 7 Results:					
Day 10 Results:					
Day 14 Results:					

If you've done the experiment correctly, here are the results you'll probably get. The avocado that had a banana with it will get ripe first and the one with the apple will ripen second. The one by itself in a brown paper bag will be ripe next, followed by the one on the kitchen counter. The last avocado to get ripe will be the one you put inside the frig. Did you guess correctly before you did the experiment?

An avocado is actually a fruit, not a vegetable. Different fruits give off varying amounts of a gas that's called ethylene gas. The avocado inside the paper bag ripened more quickly than the one on the counter because that gas was trapped inside the bag. A banana gives off that gas too so it made the avocado ripen even more quickly.

Bananas have more ethylene gas than apples do, so that's why the avocado in the bag with the banana was the fastest to ripen. You can probably guess that the cold temperatures inside the refrigerator made the release of the gas go slower, so that's the avocado that was the slowest to ripen.

SUMMARY

There are lots of fun science experiments you can do with simple foods in your kitchen. Form some hypotheses and see if your hypotheses are correct.

Always get an adult to supervise you when you do experiments at home or in school. It's fun to be a scientist in your home kitchen!

Awesome! Now that you've tried some fun experiments with food, you may want to try more fun science experiments in the Baby Professor book It's My Body, Can't You See? Science Book Experiments.

Visit

BABY PROFESSOR
EDUCATION KIDS

www.BabyProfessorBooks.com

to download Free Baby Professor eBooks
and view our catalog of new and exciting
Children's Books

9798869434630